Tra
Und...

Overcoming the Trauma Bond in a Narcissistic Relationship

By

Lauren Kozlowski

While every precaution has been taken in the preparation of this book, the publisher assumes no responsibility for errors or omissions, or for damages resulting from the use of the information contained herein.

TRAUMA BONDING: UNDERSTANDING AND OVERCOMING THE TRAUMATIC BOND IN A NARCISSISTIC RELATIONSHIP

First edition. February 2, 2020.

ISBN: 978-1393216636

Written by Lauren Kozlowski.

Table of Contents

Escapethenarcissist.com

@escapethenarcs

The Trauma Bond Test

In order to understand if this is the right book for you, I'd like to begin with a trauma bond 'test'. This will help you work out if you're in an abusive relationship and are trapped in a toxic trauma bond, or if you're still trauma bonded to an ex-spouse. Answer the following questions honestly, taking the time to think about the truth of your situation before you answer them.

You may be in the grasp of a tight trauma bond if you exhibit the following behaviors or thoughts:

- You know that your partner or ex is abusive and manipulative, but you can't seem to be able to let go of them. You give a lot of thought to the many incidents of abuse you've endured, you engage in bouts of self-blame, and the abuser is the negotiator of your self-esteem and self-worth. Despite the pain and hurt they make you feel, letting go isn't something you feel capable of.

- You often walk on eggshells in an attempt to try to appease or please your abuser. Despite the fact that they give you very little in return (apart from perhaps a few crumbs of affection), you find tiptoeing around them is something you have to do in order to keep the peace in your search for 'normality'.

- You feel like you're addicted to them. You seek out their validation and approval, and you feel like you need this from them, as it acts as a source of comfort for you. Their approval is a shelter of comfort, particularly after incidents of abuse. This indicates a strong psychological attachment to the abuser.

● You find that you defend your abuser and keep their wicked side a secret from others. You might have been in a situation where you've refused to press charges against your abuser, or you've defended them against those who tried to tell you that they're toxic. In all likelihood, you perhaps even present your relationship as a happy one to your peers and family, attempting to minimize their abusive tendencies. You may also find that you exaggerate any positive behaviors they offer out occasionally, in an attempt to show your abuser in a favorable light.

● Should you attempt to leave the abuser, you find that you always give in to the abuser's fake remorse, their pitiful crocodile tears, and their promises to change in the future. Despite the pattern of abuse and its toxic cycle being clearly evident, you grasp onto the misplaced hope that things can get better.

● You may have developed some self-sabotaging behaviors and could engage in some form of self-harm to dissociate yourself from the pain of the abuse. You may also find that you're prone to engaging in other self-sabotaging behaviors such as heavy drinking or taking drugs; this is often to mask the profound sense of shame caused by the abuse.

• You are prepared to lower your standards for this toxic person, accepting what you previously believed was unacceptable. This happens time after time, and you may find that as the abuse continues, you accept more horrific and damaging abuse each time.

• You change your behavior and personality in an attempt to meet the abuser's ever-moving goalposts, despite the fact that the abuser rarely (if ever) changes their behavior to please you.

Did some of these resonate with you? Did you read these and find that you could apply them to your own situation, or that some of my descriptions run parallel to your circumstances? If the answer is yes to any of these, then it's likely you're in the tightly wound grip of an abusive relationship, bound to your abuser by a toxic trauma bond.

It can be hard to accept the notion that you're in an abusive relationship, let alone accept the idea that you're traumatically bonded to this person; for a lengthy period of my life, I shunned the idea I was trauma bonded. Instead, I chose to believe I was pursuing the chance of happiness that I had with my abuser (although I didn't refer to him as my 'abuser' at the time). I believed I was fighting for love, and that obtaining love and happiness wasn't easy, and that the tough times with my abuser were just testing my commitment to this person.

Looking back on myself then, I can see I was merely making excuses as to why I was staying in such a toxic, nasty, hurtful, soul-crushing relationship. I didn't want to face up to the truth that I was being abused, nor did I ever want to believe that I was attached to my abuser so deeply that I would endure any amount of pain to be with him. So, instead, I maintained my stance that I was with him because I loved him, and in his own way, he loved me back.

Confusing genuine love and the trauma bond is incredibly easy to do. Lines get blurred beyond comprehension, particularly when you're in a foggy state of mind due to being treated so despicably.

If you did connect with any of the scenarios I mentioned, then I think this book can be of use to you. It'll help you understand what a trauma bond is, focusing on the bond that is developed when you're in an emotionally abusive, narcissistic relationship. It will give you a broad overview of this toxic bond and how it develops and eventually wraps around your entire being. More than this, I want to offer some advice on how you can go about breaking this toxic bond. I understand that just because you're reading this, it doesn't mean you're ready to leave your abuser yet - I know how long it took me to muster the strength to break away from my abuser. But, having the tools you need already embedded into your mind is a helpful asset to have when you come to want to sever the ties you have with your abuser.

You may have already left your abuser, but are still struggling with the trauma bond. The invisible cord that ties you to them isn't so easily cut, and simply leaving the relationship isn't always enough to snip that malignant thread that's tethered to you. If this is your situation, then this book can help you get a deeper understanding of why it's so difficult to let go, as well as offering you some 'survival' tips on your journey to recovering from a trauma bond.

What is Trauma Bonding to a Narcissist?

So far, you've ascertained that you may be in a trauma bond with a narcissist, or you may feel certain that you are. The first step to overcoming this is to understand just what it is that's entrapping you and keeping you in such a hurtful relationship.

The Beginning

Oftentimes when I'm talking to other victims of narcissistic abuse and the subsequent trauma bond, I hear about the survivor experiencing mixed feelings for their partner who behaves so abusively. I can absolutely resonate with this - it's like a mental game of tug of war. The abuser completely has your heart in their grasp, but it appears there's always a little shred of logic and rationale that they didn't manage to capture. It's this glimmer of reason that tries to fight against the bond and creates an internal war of heart versus head. Of course, we both know which one wins most of the time.

It's entirely valid to still feel love and care for someone who you've invested so much time and energy into building a relationship with. As you can likely agree, it wasn't the abusive behavior and hurtful words and actions that ignited your attraction to begin with. Being told you're worthless, or stupid, or never going to meet anyone else probably didn't stir up feelings of love and adoration. Even after the nasty and abusive behaviors begin, we believe that leaning towards these feelings of love, compassion, and care will help us cope with the verbal abuse or violence (even if it's just in the short-term). That being said, logic also allows us to know that abusive behaviors tend to escalate over time, so using these emotions and thoughts as coping mechanisms can have damaging impacts in the long-term. But, as I mentioned before, logic isn't something that tends to win in the battle of heart versus head.

A lot of survivors of narcissistic abuse who have opened up to me also tell me that their abusive spouse exhibited 'good' or 'nice' behaviors too. Many of these survivors commented to me that their partners were or are 'perfect' the majority of the time and that it's just a small percentage of the time that they're abusive or problematic. This wasn't the case for me, however, nor was it the case for plenty of other survivors I'd spoken to, but it did reveal to me that the scale of abuse is very different for each relationship. Some victims endure it almost every day - they'll wake up with a sick feeling in the pit of their stomach, unsure as to how the day will pan out. Will they be abused today? Will they be screamed at, told they're pathetic, will they be berated for not doing something to their abuser's liking? Others may endure this toxic behavior much less, but when it happens, it completely throws their entire being off-kilter. Either way, a toxic trauma bond can be formed, and regardless of the frequency of abuse, it's just as hard to handle.

For me, the abuse was what felt like a constant stream of toxicity. It was a never-ending barrage of being told I was worthless, being emotionally and physically abused, and feeling undeserving of my existence. Through this horrible toxic fog, I would sometimes get glimmers of the man I met. The funny one, the loving one, the one who made me happy. Though these instances were few and far between, and I craved them so much, they were actually part of a calculated plan on his part. What I've learned through the course of me educating myself on narcissistic abuse is that the positive behaviors offered by the narcissist are to actually enable the abusive behaviors to continue and eventually escalate. This is because the 'good' behaviors exhibited make it so hard for victims to follow through with the impulse to leave when horrific abuse occurs. If your partner was abusive all the time, constantly evil towards you 24/7, and never kind or pleasant towards you, it would be so much easier for you to up and leave. The good behavior they show, in other words, is what nurtures the toxic attachment that makes getting away from the abuse, no matter how horrific or violent or emotionally shattering, feel so painful and difficult.

This cycle, in which the abuser cycles between abuse and non-abuse (violent or emotional, or both) while the victim simply copes with it, demonstrates the basic components of the trauma bond.

To better understand the formula behind this damaging attachment to a spouse who behaves abusively, I'll break down the science of the bond. This will also help expose to you the dangers ingrained in it, which can be hard to hear when you're in the clutches of an abuser. For years, I buried my head in the sand, refusing to accept that I was bonded to such a harmful person. I didn't want to feel weak, stupid, or like I'd made idiotic choices, which is how those around had made me feel. To accept the notion that I was trauma bonded seemed to only serve to validate their thoughts of me and my situation. However, when I did delve deeper into educating myself on trauma bonding, I found there was a science to it, and this helped lift some of the blame and guilt from me.

The Science of the Bond

Talking biologically, the bonds we develop in life originate from our infantile dependence on someone else for our survival, which is usually our primary caregiver: our parent.

Survival is the primal foundation of human attachment, so when our safety is threatened, i.e., by trauma, we naturally turn to someone who is seen as the caregiver in our lives, someone who offers support, and provides protection, and care. When this type of bonding occurs, oxytocin (which is often called the love hormone for its role in reproduction) is released into our brains, promoting comfort and attachment with the caregiver. This then develops in adult relationships, where the 'caregiver' is usually our significant other.

Hopefully, this stripped-down science lesson can help you see how trauma bonds occur - when the person who we regard as our significant other, or the 'caregiver,' is also the one creating our trauma by threatening our safety through their abusive behavior towards us. Because we are all essentially wired from birth to turn towards an attachment figure when we feel under threat, we instinctively turn to our spouse when abuse occurs, despite the fact that they are the one who is being abusive to us. This then leads to us feeling bonded to them.

As humans, we also have a tendency to try to make sense of our experiences, so we work exceptionally hard to rationalize the disharmony between our abusive partner's caring behavior and their harmful actions towards us. This attempt at rationalization strengthens the toxic bond further. To add to all that, abusive partners will often promise to change and will manipulatively tend to the very wounds they created, exactly at those moments when we are most exposed, vulnerable, and hurt.

For example, my abuser made sure I severed contact with family and friends, leaving me alone and incredibly isolated. This isolation would then mean I'd be dependant upon my spouse for human interaction and would reach out for him when I felt most alone. He would sometimes be a great source of comfort for my feelings of isolation, despite him being the reason I was so secluded from everything I once held so dear in life.

He would also be the reason for great insecurities I had, such as making me feel inferior to other women, or like I was too stupid to apply for job roles I'd always dreamed of doing one day. In the same breath, he'd be the place I'd turn for comfort over these depressing insecurities and fears, not accepting he was the reason they'd manifested originally.

It is no wonder that we end up feeling so strongly connected to them and have an incredibly difficult time imagining life without them. This then spawns a new hurdle to overcome: the dangers of being exposed to the abuse and the tightening of the trauma bond.

The Danger of the Bond

The true danger of traumatic bonding lies in the horrific impact that repeated trauma has on us. Whilst some effects are more glaring and recognizable, such as marks from physical abuse, others may be less noticeable. Either way, the more abuse we face, the deeper the bond tends to set within us. The deeper the bond, the more we are entangled in the abuser's clutches, leaving us with the feeling of hopelessness.

One common side effect of experiencing abusive behavior is the overproduction of cortisol, which is nature's very own built-in alarm. This is normally released to provide us with much-needed energy when we're faced with stress, but too much cortisol can end up damaging our immune system and make us more likely to pick up an illness, become more anxious, and can also create high blood pressure. When I first found this out, it made sense; through the years I was with my abuser, I was forever poorly. From always having a common cold to aches and pains in my muscles, to having a constant headache, this was all down to the abuse I was enduring. At the time, I put it down to me simply being 'sickly', which isn't something I'd ever been in my life. I'd resigned myself to always having a dull headache, which often spawned into a throbbing migraine. It was only a few months after leaving my abuser did I wake up without a dull ache in my temples or an ache behind my eyes - for the first time in years and years. It was like I could almost *see* again after being blind; whilst that sounds like a dramatic analogy, it was a euphoric moment when I felt what I should have felt all along. The headache came back again later that day, but as time went on, the foggy headaches and migraines slowly lifted. Now, I can't recall the last time I suffered a migraine (touch wood!)

As well as the physical marks that can be left or the dangerous overproduction of cortisol, there is a lot of other health concerns that can result from enduring abuse. From physical ailments like asthma and fibromyalgia to mental and emotional afflictions such as traumatic flashbacks and depression, being exposed to repeated trauma can impact our health in often surprising ways.

I hope this has helped you understand the trauma bond a bit more, and offered an explanation as to why you and I (or anyone else for that matter) would stay in an abusive relationship. The bond, as I've mentioned, is greater than logic. Unfortunately, the bond is also more complex than most people can comprehend (or want to try and understand), which can make you feel incredibly alone and powerless to do anything about it. Hopefully, knowing I've been there myself, as have many other survivors, can help you feel alleviated of at least some feelings of confusion you may have.

With that in mind, I'd like to enter the next chapter of the book, in which I want to explain the stages that lead to trauma bonding, which will give you further understanding of your emotions towards your abuser.

The Seven Stages that Lead to You Becoming Trauma Bonded

As I touched upon earlier, you don't enter a relationship with a wicked monster who seems to revel in you feeling low and miserable, as someone who wants to strip you of your sense of self-worth. If your spouse had shown you their nasty traits the first time you met them, you wouldn't be in this position now - you'd have run a mile. You wouldn't have entered what you thought was a relationship that could go places; you'd have said 'thanks, but no thanks' and removed yourself from the threat of an abusive partnership.

However, this isn't how it works with any abuser, particularly a manipulative narcissist.

You also don't enter the relationship and suddenly become 'trauma bonded'. Like anything with the narcissist, it's carefully planned and executed, and there is a process to you becoming toxically bonded and emotionally dependant on your abuser.

This tends to happen in seven stages, give or take, and you'll find that whilst all of the stages seemed like a natural, toxic progression, they were all very methodically calculated. The aim of these stages is to eventually keep you in the clutches of the narcissist, and what better way to keep you than a trauma bond? After all, the end goal for a narcissist is complete control, and that precisely what a trauma bind can afford them.

Stage 1: Love Bombing - The narc will shower you with love, affection, attention, and validation.

Love bombing is a tactic used by the narcissist to draw you into their cat-trap. Often they seem too perfect to be true, and the beginning of the relationship is almost fairy-tale like. They seem to dote on you, and you feel utterly adored and cared for. The abundance of love and affection you received during this first phase is like nothing you've ever experienced before.

From experience, being love-bombed is unlike any other 'honeymoon period' you see in a healthy 'dating' situation, whereas most people will hold back and give little pieces of affection and vulnerability as they continue to date, a narcissist will offer this almost straight away. Most people will hold back a little, not only to protect themselves and make sure they are dating the right kind of person but also to refrain from scaring their potential partner away. Not a narcissist.

They will declare their love, obsession, and affection in the early stages of the relationship. Narcissists often pick their prey based on the characteristics they exhibit; an empathetic, kind, and trusting individual is like gold dust to them. Naturally, someone who is an emotionally open, empathetic, and trusting person won't question someone's motives when they declare their adoration and love.

Stage 2: Trust and Dependency - You begin to trust that they will love you unconditionally, always. You now start to depend on them for validation.

The abundance of love bombing can only result in gaining your trust, which the narc knows, develops into a dependency. Healthy love and a healthy dependency are part of a nurturing relationship, but the kind of dependency the narcissist manifests in you is entirely unhealthy.

You begin to trust them so much that their opinion becomes the one source of validation that you care about, which is where the next stage takes effect.

Stage 3: The Criticism Begins - The narcissist gradually reduces the amount of care and validation that they once gave you. They start to criticize you place heavy blame on you for things you have no control over. Their demanding side really comes out.

This stage is where the abuse is really ramped up to something that hurts, demeans, and belittles you. Before this, the narcissist was a sturdy source of support and comfort, and now they're pulling away from you emotionally. This makes you feel like you're going insane; the thought of losing them is beyond gut-wrenching.

What makes this even more painful is the criticism, nasty comments, and blame that they begin to heap upon you. Because this is so foreign, and your spouse had always been so 'good' to you, you believe that what they're saying is absolutely true. You don't understand this at the time, but you believing their hurtful comments is something the narcissist banks on - after all, they need to chip away at your morale and self-esteem to reach stage 4.

Stage 4: Gaslighting - The narcissist will tell you that their unhappiness is all your fault. If you would only do exactly as they say, they would be able to love you like they used to. They will aim to make you doubt your own perception of reality and want you to accept their interpretation of reality.

Gaslighting could be a whole book of its own; it's such a nasty, toxic, crazy-making form of manipulation, and I have enough experience of this to fill a book twice over. Gaslighting, at its poisonous core, is the way the narcissist uses psychological manipulation to make their victim into doubt their own sanity.

If you've ever been told, 'I didn't say that! You always make up things,' or 'You've got it wrong again, that didn't happen!', or 'You definitely told me this,' despite you knowing the truth of the situation, you've been exposed to this form of manipulation. I've been told I've said and done things that I knew deep down didn't happen, but when you're being consistently gaslighted, you begin to believe the narc's version of events over your own sanity. It sounds almost unbelievable that someone else can hold this type of mental control over you, but it's entirely possible, and it's a horribly poisonous form of abuse.

Stage 5: Control is Set - You feel like your only chance of getting back to the happy, comforting feelings of Stage 1 is to do things the narc's way.

You so desperately want to be back at stage 1; you want to be adored, loved, cared for, told you're special, perfect, you want to feel like you're important again. The narc knows this.

They also know that you'll do what they say in the glimmer of hope that they'll return to the love bomber they once were. They'll dangle this like a carrot in front of you, making sure they get what they want from you in return for that slight sliver of hope that they'll revert to adoring you again.

Stage 6: Loss of Self - Things get worse, not better - and you resign yourself to accepting their abuse. Should you fight back, they will intensify their abuse. Stage 6 is where you are entirely confused, miserable, and your self-esteem is at an all-time low.

I find this the most heartbreaking of all the stages because this is the point you become a shell of a being; you're alive and breathing, but you're an emotional corpse, feeling dead inside. Compare the person you are at stage 6 to the person you were before you met your abuser - it's like night and day.

Dreams, hopes, goals, and desires become mute at this point. You no longer have any. The one thing you want is for the abuse to stop, and you'll do anything for that to happen, even if it means doing things you don't want to do (at the narc's request). Stage 6 is a dangerous place to be, and this is where I contemplated my existence on this planet. I'd endured so much abuse torment and violence that I didn't see any other way out, and it's such a pitiful and painful place to be.

Stage 7: Addiction - Your family and friends are concerned about you. You feel terrible about this situation, but you cannot leave because your abuser is now everything to you. All you can think about is winning their affections and validation.

At this point, it's highly probable that you're cut off from your family and friends, but that doesn't stop you feeling awful about not seeing them. Even if it was your choice to cut them off, it's likely that it was the narc that was the driving force behind that. You may miss your family, friends, and the life you left behind for your abuser, and the guilt and shame you feel about that can often be all-consuming.

This is what the narc has strived for all along - your addiction to them. This means they have the power and control they strived for all along, and they know pretty much nothing and nobody can take you away from them. They can hurt you, cheat, lie, and act unashamedly toxic and you'll still stick around and endure it. This is the end goal achieved for the narcissist.

You may be asking yourself, much like I did, how it's possible that this can happen to you? A sane, logical, intelligent, and functional person like you?

The answer to this question is the same for all of us who've endured such abuse. It comes from understanding the core dynamics of how we humans react to the combination of dependency and abuse coupled with something called 'intermittent reinforcement'. I'll delve a little deeper into intermittent reinforcement because I think it'll help you connect the dots as to why people like us stay in such abusive and toxic relationships for such a long time.

Intermittent Reinforcement

To help piece together how intermittent reinforcement keeps us in the clutches of a trauma bond, I'll mention a study carried out that proves the power of intermittent reinforcement. The study aimed to get healthy lab rats to keep pressing a bar in the hope that they would keep on getting pellets of food. The goal of this study was to keep the rats working for the food rewards long after they had stopped receiving any. They chose lab rats because, apparently, they react in a similar way to humans in this kind of situation.

The researchers tried various patterns of rewards and found the following:

Pattern #1 - Reward the rats every time they press the bar

This turned out to be the least effective reward pattern. The rats soon expected to be rewarded after every time they touched the bar. When the food rewards eventually stopped, the rats may press the bar one or two more times just to try their luck and see if any new food pellets appeared. However, after a short while, all of the rats quickly wandered away and no longer paid any attention to the bar.

Pattern #2—The rats get rewarded for every 10th press of the bar

For pattern number 2, the researchers got the rats accustomed to pressing the bar a total of 10 times before any food was given. This meant the rats could not gather that no more food would come until they'd had already done the work of pressing the bar at least 10 times. Most rats tried at least one more round of bar touches and did another set of 10. However, it didn't take too long for all the rats to realize there would be no more food rewards for their efforts, and they stopped working and went to look elsewhere for food.

Pattern #3 - Food would be rewarded every 10 minutes

For this pattern, the rats learned that they would only get their food pellets on a set time schedule. Once they came to understand that they would always get rewarded 10 minutes after a bar press, they became very frugal with their presses. They tended to press the bar once or twice towards the end of the 10-minute waiting period, then wait for their pellets. After the rewards completely stopped, it only took a few non-rewarded 10-minutes for the rats to stop expecting the food and move on. The learning from this pattern was that having a predictable pattern of rewards for pressing the bar seen fewer bar presses after once the food had stopped being given.

Pattern #4 - Intermittent Reinforcement

This is the pattern that saw the researchers finally outwit the rats by completely scrapping any predictable pattern of rewarding. They randomized the times between rewards and moved the goalposts as to how many bar presses would be needed to get food pellets in exchange for their work. What's fascinating about this test is that the rats kept pressing the bar, even though they were never rewarded for doing so again.

The hopeful response of bar pressing was never stopped on a reward schedule of intermittent reinforcement. The rats continued to work in anticipation that eventually they would once again be rewarded.

Much like the hopeful rats in this study, we will continue to try and please our abuser in the hope that this will be recognized and we will be rewarded with their love. And, much like the researchers in this study, the narcissist knows that randomizing their attention and moving their goalposts will make you strive harder for their bread crumbs of affection. Not only that, but you won't give up or lose interest, because intermittent reinforcement leaves you hoping that the next reward is just around the corner - even if it isn't.

The aim of this chapter was to help you see that the abuser utilizes their manipulative mind games in order to get you where they want you - I want to help rationalize any shame or guilt you may feel about getting involved in an abusive relationship. I know the pitiful feelings of embarrassment and humiliation when people say, 'Why don't you just leave if your relationship is bad?' or 'Why did you stay in an abusive relationship for so long? If that was me, I'd of left at the first sign of trouble'. After hearing such ignorant and blameful questions, I'd go away and mull over their probing and try to answer their hurtful questions in my head. Of course, the resolution I'd always come up with was that I was weak, stupid, and must have deserved such horrific abuse.

However, that was the effects of the abuse talking, and once I began my research on the abuse I'd endured, it came as a weight lifted off my shoulders when I found out about the biological reasoning for trauma bonding. Couple this with the seven stages of entrapment the abuser utilizes and the use of intermittent reinforcement by the narcissist, and you have a recipe for complete control.

Whilst it's hard to accept that someone would want to hurt you and cause you pain so intentionally, it's a burden lifted once you realize that you're not to blame for the abuse, nor are you to blame for sticking by your abuser.

This leads me to my next topic, which is Stockholm Syndrome. Trauma bonding and Stockholm Syndrome have a lot of similarities, and the symptoms and methods used by the abuser often run parallel to that of trauma bonding. For a while, I went through a phase of really researching this topic and reading up on cases of victims who had Stockholm Syndrome. This was because it resonated with me so much; I could connect with their feelings and emotions and their reasons for making the choices they made.

Whilst explaining the full ins and outs of Stockholm Syndrome goes beyond the scope of this book, I think delving deeper into this subject is a good way to exorcise any demons of guilt or shame you hold about being caught in the grip of a tight trauma bond.

A Look at Stockholm Syndrome and its Parallels to Trauma Bonding

Stockholm syndrome is something that develops when people find themselves in a situation where they have an intense fear of harm physical injury and believe that all control is solely in the hands of their abuser. The psychological response that follows this, after a period of time, is an instinctive survival strategy for the victim. It shows the abused individual offering sympathy and support for their abuser's plight and can even begin to feel negative feelings toward those who are trying to help remove the victim from the situation. Circumstances in which victims have shown this kind of response include those who have been held hostage, long-term kidnappings, those who have been a member of a cult, and even prisoners of war.

To give a quick summary of Stockholm syndrome, in order for you to compare its similarities to trauma bonding, I'll give you some quick takeaways about the condition:

> • People who exhibit the symptoms of Stockholm syndrome often become very protective of their captors or abusers, even in some cases where they've foiled the authorities' efforts to rescue them. I recall when the police turned up to the house I lived at with my abusive ex after being called by a 'concerned neighbor' (that's why the police told us they were there). The police asked to speak to me alone away

from my ex, which I could tell made him extremely angry, but he obliged to leave the room whilst the police asked me questions. Despite his nice demeanor to the offices, I could tell the police saw right through him and knew the reality of the situation - that I was a victim. The police did the best they could to coax some truth out of me, but even though I was alone with them, I wouldn't open up and tell them how my partner was emotionally and physically abusive. In fact, as went as far as to tell them how happy I was and how shocked I was that they'd been called out (I can only imagine how see-through my lies were at the time). At the time, things like coercive control weren't as understood as they are these days - in short, the police had to take what I was saying at face value, regardless of what they could see or what their instincts were telling them about the situation. They ended their questioning of me by saying, 'It's clear that you're not ready to open up - but we're here when you need us.' This parting comment made me feel undeniably weak even though the officer who said it only meant to help. I actively sabotaged the effort that people were making to help me, much like someone suffering from Stockholm syndrome. I knew that I was lying to protect my abuser, and I knew he was cruel and vile towards me, but at the time, there was no way I was going to tell the truth about the abuse I was enduring. It wasn't necessarily out of fear, either; I cared about my ex, and I didn't want anything bad to happen to him. Again, this feeling of loyalty runs parallel with that of someone who has Stockholm syndrome.

● The syndrome is not actually a named disease - you won't find this in any manual. It's rather a way to describe the behaviors of those who've been repeatedly traumatized over a period of time.

● Whilst it's commonly reported that hostages and kidnapping victims exhibit the behaviors associated with the syndrome, so can people who are (or have been) in abusive relationships or a member of a cult.

● The name 'Stockholm syndrome' originated from a 1973 bank robbery in Stockholm, Sweden, where four hostages were held for a total of six days. During their imprisonment, and fully in the firing line of harm, the hostages seemed to defend the actions of their captors. The captives even seemed to scold efforts by the government to rescue them from the situation. They pled with the authorities for their captors not to be harmed during the rescue and engineered ways for that to happen. Following the incident, and after being rescued, the victims couldn't explain their feelings of sympathy and lack of anger toward their captors. Months after their hostage ordeal had ended, the victims of the bank robbery were continuing to show their loyalty to the robbers. They refused to testify against them and helped the robbers raise funds for legal fees. They even went as far as to visit them whilst they were in prison. This just goes to show how powerful the bond that Stockholm syndrome creates is, much like the all-consuming bond that can manifest in a narcissistic relationship.

I think the syndrome is fascinating, not only because I find it comparable with my own situation, but because it goes to show the power a human being can have over another, and the irrational and illogical behaviors it incites from the victims. The fact that Stockholm syndrome is a survival mechanism really intrigues me, and researching this topic after I'd endured similar symptoms was something I found enlightening and cathartic. The behaviors of those with Stockholm syndrome didn't intrigue just me, either; it's caught the attention of researchers who wanted to know more about the bond you can form with a captor after the Stockholm incident became worldwide news. The supportive and empathetic bond that was created in the Swedish bank robbery spawned curiosity from psychologists, too - one psychologist who'd been involved with the Stockholm hostage situation was the person to actually coin the term 'Stockholm Syndrome,' and another clearly defined it so that the FBI and Scotland Yard (and the officers that worked in those organizations) would be able to understand that it's an entirely possible aspect of a hostage situation. The subsequent studies of the condition helped then execute their negotiations in future incidents of a similar nature.

You may be wondering what *causes* Stockholm syndrome? You already understand the trauma bond in an abusive relationship, and how that slowly manifests and grows into a toxic control trap. But for Stockholm syndrome, again, it's very similar to the trauma bond as to what emotions cause it to happen. Albeit the circumstances are often more extreme in Stockholm syndrome scenarios (life or death, usually), thus speeding up the symptoms of the syndrome, but the reasoning behind the bond is quite close to home:

The victim will believe that their captor can and will kill them. The feeling of relief is felt by the victim for not being killed. This will then turn into gratitude.

Isolation from anyone but the captors engenders the intense feelings of dependency.

The victim will believe that escaping is an impossibility.

The victim will also inflate the captor's acts of kindness into a genuine care for each other's wellbeing.

Victims of the syndrome tend to suffer from severe isolation as well as emotional and physical abuse from the captor. As you know, isolation and abuse are also demonstrated in the situations of battered spouses, emotional abuse victims, as well as abused children - each of these circumstances can up with the victim or victims responding in an extremely compliant and supportive way as a method for survival.

As an aside, I found out that people with Stockholm syndrome tend to show some of the same symptoms as those who have post-traumatic stress syndrome (also known as PTSD - something else I was interested in as it also included a lot of the symptoms I exhibited after my relationship ended). These symptoms included insomnia, recurring nightmares, great difficulty concentrating, a deep distrust of others, frequently in a state of confusion, an overly sensitive startle reflex, and a loss of interest and excited in (what were) favorite activities. Both of these syndromes and trauma bonding have a great deal in common, so I've found it somewhat cathartic to delve deeper into all of these topics.

Famous Cases of Stockholm Syndrome (that you may have heard of but didn't realize the victim suffered from the syndrome)

The year that followed the Stockholm bank incident, the syndrome became widely known by the masses because of a woman named Patty Hearst.

Patty Hearst, at the young age of 19, was kidnapped by the Symbionese Liberation Army. A couple of months after her kidnapping, she was photographed participating in an SLA bank robbery. After this, a tape recording was released with Patty (her SLA pseudonym was Tania) expressing her support for and commitment to the SLA's cause. After the group, including Patty, were all arrested, she rejected the radical group.

During her trial, her defense attributed her behavior during her time with the SLA to a subconscious way to survive, comparing her behavior in captivity to other victims of Stockholm syndrome. During her time in captivity, Hearst said she had been bound, blindfolded, and kept in a small closet, where she was abused (both physically and sexually) for weeks leading up to the bank robbery.

On June 10, 1991, **Jaycee Lee Dugard** was abducted by a school bus stop near where she lived in South Lake Tahoe, California. Her mysterious disappearance remained unsolved until August 27, 2009, when she entered a police station in California and introduced herself as the missing girl (or woman, as she now was).

For a total of 18 years, she was held hostage in a tent right behind the home of her captors, Phillip and Nancy Garrido. It was there that Dugard gave birth to two children, who were aged 15 and 11 at the time of her reappearance. It transpired that the opportunity to escape was present at different times throughout her time in captivity, but Jaycee Dugard had bonded with her captors as a way of survival, which left her unable to capitalize on the chances she had to escape.

Another high profile case you may have heard of is **Natascha Kampusch**, who, in August 2006, managed to escape from her kidnapper, Wolfgang Priklopil. He had kept her locked in a small cell for over eight years. She stayed in that windowless cell, which was 54 square feet, for her first six months of captivity. As time went by, she was eventually permitted to be in the main house, where she would then cook and clean for her captor.

After several years of captivity, she was allowed out into the garden area occasionally. At one point, she was even introduced to her kidnapper's business partner, who described her as being relaxed and happy. Priklopil controlled Kampusch in a number of ways; he'd starve her in order to make her physically weak, he'd severely beat her and threatened to kill her and his neighbors if she tried to escape him. After Kampusch finally did escape, Priklopi ended his own life by jumping in front of a train. When Kampusch discovered that Priklopil was dead, she cried, apparently inconsolably, and even lit a candle for him.

In a documentary based on her book, she said of her captor, "he's a poor soul."

Loving a narcissist is like Stockholm Syndrome. I'm not saying trauma bonding and the syndrome are the same thing, but they run some very close parallels, and knowing about Stockholm syndrome can help you understand the power of control in an abusive situation.

Just like the hostage victims describe above, leaving an abuser or an abusive relationship is not easy. Abusive relationships are, just like the relationship between captor and captive, complex and traumatic. The cycle of abuse is prevalent and undeniably difficult to break free from, let alone get over. We become so painfully addicted to a relationship and person who is pure poison to us. It's like a drug for so many of us who've endured this type of experience. The only person who can make you feel good again is the person who is hurting you.

The 5 Stages of Accepting You're Trauma Bonded

The only way to free ourselves from the clutches of an abusive relationship is to take all the energy that's being wasted on the abuser and focus it back on ourselves. To free yourself is to find the strength to take your focus off trying to fix them, appease them, pacify or change them. Change yourself instead.

As I began to strive to work on my self-esteem, I started to realize that I deserved better. I mean a genuine, profound realization that I really, truly deserved to be treated better. The more I worked on me and my own feelings and needs, I accepted that this relationship simply wasn't good enough for me. I had to leave (I'll go into detail about this a little later in the book). I had to plan to leave when I felt ready to do so - it's not as black and white as making a plan and leaving immediately in most cases. You need to muster up the will to do so first. Only then can you heal.

Leaving an abusive relationship is one of the hardest things you will ever do in your life. I left and returned to my ex multiple times, even after the abuse only ever escalates and gets viler each time. I'd leave the relationship with a resolve to leave for good, only for it to melt away when he clicked his fingers again. Here you see the trauma bond working its toxic magic yet again.

The majority of other victims that I've talked to say the same. They tell me that they metally minimize what they've endured and what's gone on through the relationship. That once the bruises fade, the relationship doesn't seem so bad after all. They felt, much like I did for so many years, that perhaps they had overreacted to what had happened to them. They felt immense guilt for abandoning their abuser when they 'needed' them.

Victims who go onto become survivors of an abusive relationship progress through a process of 5 stages before finally breaking free from the restraints of a toxic relationship. The first stages are when we are still in the relationship.

I went through every one of these stages I'll describe, and I've discussed these stages with other survivors, too, and we're in agreement: these stages are like a bereavement of sorts. You're going through some similar emotions and mental shifts as you grieve the loss of the life you thought you would have, as well the person you thought loved you.

Stage #1: Denial

This is where we deny and /or minimize the abuse we've endured. Despite everyone around being able to see what's going on, we seem to lack awareness of how bad it truly is. In reality, we're simply denying what's happening and trying to minimize its toxic influence on us. During this stage, which is where most people stay for a very long time, we feel trapped and utterly hopeless to improve things. Sadly, we make no genuine attempts to take action to make our lives safer or less threatening.

Instead of viewing our spouse as the nasty, abusive, soul-crushing individual they've turned out to be, we prefer to see them as the person we first met, who love-bombed us and made us feel so wanted and special. The good times, and the 'honeymoon stage' after an incident of abuse, is what we prefer to associate with our abuser - not their viciously nasty true self. We ache to believe their promises that it won't happen again. In turn, we manage to delude ourselves into thinking that if we work to please them and not provoke or upset them, the abuse will stop.

If others question any bruises or any red flags of abuse, we'll make up excuses on the spot. Many of us seem to be exceptionally good at doing that, but I often struggled to be totally convincing - my face and what I was saying never matched. Nevertheless, I'd still make up excuses and false reasons as to why I had marks on my body or why my partner seemed to be controlling. I'd say anything if it stopped any blame being aimed toward him. I was so scared of losing him.

At this point, the fear of losing my partner made me feel like I just loved him too much to leave; I wasn't yet aware that I was trauma bonded. However, during Stage 1, we are still in a state of absolute denial, and to think we are part of an unhealthy attachment isn't something we are willing to comprehend.

We can't yet face the idea that we've become dependent on the same person who is hurting us. We won't be able to consider the notion that we need them to make us feel good after abuse.

During Stage 1, we are able to numb our real emotions. Of course, we feel hurt, pain, rejection, and all of the negative things the narcissist wants us to, but we numb the emotions we'd need to feel in order to listen to our gut instincts. This only accentuates our profuse denial. We genuinely believe our own rationalizations and come to trust that the abuse isn't as bad as it is.

The narc's manipulative tactics are also cleverly designed to make us accept responsibility for their vile behavior. We internalize this blame and rationalize that: *If I hadn't done this, they wouldn't have got so angry with me. Had I not said that the abuse wouldn't have happened in the first place.*

We feel completely and utterly feel helpless. So very trapped. But still, we also refrain from letting on about how bad things are - this will remain hidden from others. I didn't reach out for help for such a long, long time, and it's a huge regret of mine.

Until you are able to admit there is a problem, you can't take steps to change it. At this point, you are convinced that you can help them to change by changing what you do and say to meet their desires. As long as you keep changing your behavior and taking on the responsibility for theirs, you're fruitlessly hanging onto the hope that things will one day be okay. You stay in the relationship forever waiting and praying for it to improve. But it only gets worse.

Stage #2: Admitting your reality.

You can't stay in Stage 1 forever. Stage 2 will come eventually, and when it does, you start to admit to yourself the reality of what you have been denying and minimizing for so long. This often comes when you start to become more open about finding out more about abusive relationships, such as reading books, articles, and searching the web for answers. At first, this seeking out of information is done so you can work on the relationship and find out what you need to do in order to restore it back to 'normality'. However, after delving a little deeper into the topic, your mind becomes open to the reality of the situation.

Admitting that my life was filled to the brim with abuse and toxicity was one of the most difficult steps I had to take. For a while, although I was able to acknowledge the severity of what I was enduring, I was still emotionally paralyzed, genuinely feeling unable to take steps to change my fate.

Your feelings will shift back and forth from realizing you are a victim of abuse to the denial of it and back again. You adore and crave their good side, but you fear the bad. You feel like you're on an emotional rollercoaster, unable to fund a way for it to stop. It's an extremely confusing time.

The thought of leaving still absolutely terrifies you. Even though they're hurting you, you can't bear to lose the person you love. Such conflicting feelings cause a great deal of inner turmoil and battling thoughts. I still loved my ex despite coming to understand that I was in an abusive relationship. I just wished more than anything else that the abuse would go away for good. I chose for a long time to wait it out and hope he'd change.

Some of us might fear harassment or stalking should they leave their abusive partner. A lot of us fear being left financially destitute, feeling unable to get a job. The overwhelming fear of having to start over again can be paralyzing, particularly if it involves moving away or going into hiding.

At this Stage, the fears of leaving outweigh the risks of staying in the relationship. Still, there's a big gap between the (often highly exaggerated) memories of the good times and the all-too-painful reality of how toxic the relationship is. Even after my ex almost was so violent, he put me in the hospital, I still managed to convince myself that things would one day be okay. But, gradually, the balance tips the other way. Stage 1 and 2 can soon evaporate into the cloud of acceptance, and we are able to move onto the next stage.

Stage #3: Preparing to leave

When we realize that enduring the hurtful status quo means we put ourselves (and any children who are involved in the relationship) in danger, we are able to move onto Stage 3. We become acutely aware that we have no other choice but to leave. If we don't, the abuse will only escalate more and more. Worst case scenario, we risk losing our lives. Towards the end of my relationship, the escalating violence became more aggressive, more prolonged, and the rage in his eyes became more prevalent.

Be under no illusion, however; a lot of people never reach this Stage. They fluctuate between Stage 1 and 2, knowing they're in a toxic situation and then letting denial cushion them from that reality - then rinse and repeat. The jump from Stage 2 to 3 is a big one, a difficult one, but a very important one.

This was no different for me. I found this Stage hard. I had to see my partner for who he really was, not the idealized person I had projected onto him. Not the one I was waiting for and praying he'd eventually become. By this point, I'd learned that I had to accept the things I couldn't change. Which was him - my partner. My children's father. My abuser.

I had to muster the courage to change what I could - to take control of the things I had influence over. Which was me. I had to let go of wanting to save my abuser, of wanting to rescue him from his toxic ways. I had to refocus on me.

I remember when it eventually dawned on me that I needed to accept him for who he was right now. Not who I prayed he might become one day in the future. Why would he change into the kind, loving, caring, thoughtful person I had in my head? That person, who love bombed me at the beginning of the relationship, was long gone for me. That charming, adoring man was only reserved for his other women and future victims. I knew I had to leave. My safety, my sanity, and my the wellbeing of my children finally outweighed my denial. As hard as it was, I had clarity for the first time in a long time.

Stage #4: Leaving.

This is, without a shadow of a doubt, an enormous step to take. It's the emotional culmination of having to challenge your inner fears over your future, your crippling doubts that things aren't as bad as they appear to be. Staring down the uncertainty and insecurity as to whether you are making the right decision. Constantly questioning yourself over what will happen, to you as well as them, if you take this step. Leaving, even just thinking about doing so, can cause a great deal of anxiety. When I first got to this Stage, I couldn't eat, I barely slept, I was in a state of constant anxiety the entire time. Knowing what I needed to do but being uncertain I could pull it off almost ruined me.

Often, it takes another horrific incident, following a quiet time of abuse (and usually the false promise that it will never ever happen again) that finally snaps you into leaving. I describe my leaving a bit more in-depth in my book *Narcissistic Ex*, but as you are probably already all too aware, this Stage requires a ton of strength and resolve. As does Stage 5:

Stage #5: Maintaining your strength

You need to stay strong. You have to maintain the strides you've made by leaving behind a hurtful relationship that was filled with injury, toxicity, fears, heartache, and pain. Of course, that's certainly easier said than done. People think that when you leave an abusive relationship that that's it, it's done, it's over, it's the end. But it's not.

It's just the beginning of a journey filled with healing, some difficult confrontations with the past, and a brand new future in front of you. In some ways, this can be the most painful part to comprehend.

This is the point – should you gather enough fight and strength within you – where you have finally ended an abusive relationship, grieved its death, and began life anew, safely and securely.

I got there. It was one of the toughest things I have ever done in my life. It took me a long time to understand why I was even remotely attracted to the type of person who would hurt me the way he did. I found a lot of self-hatred when questioning why I stayed with him when others wouldn't have. I had some trouble building my self-esteem to a point where I was able to maintain healthy boundaries in all aspects of my life. But I got there.

This journey, whilst difficult, was also such an empowering one. I not only found the self-confidence and self-esteem I lost whilst in the relationship, but I also went on to find new friends who I would never have made if I'd stayed with my ex. I could partake in social activities with my friends and co-workers, which was out of the question with my ex. I could buy whatever clothing I wanted to, and not be told to return it or that I couldn't wear it. I eventually found the courage to say what I was thinking; I didn't mull over what I was going to say before I said it out of fear of reprisal. I was free.

The Cognitive Dissonance That a Trauma Bond Brings

Exploitative relationships create toxic bonds, and that bond can often remain (if not exorcized properly) well after the relationship has ended. Despite years of research about the horribly damaging effects of trauma and abuse and the fact that victims will often go back to their abusers many times before they finally leave for good, society still doesn't seem to understand the powerfully shattering effects of trauma bonding can cause. It takes a victim an average of 7 times before they leave their abuser for good, but I can admit (as well as many other people whom I've spoken to can attest to this), I feel the true statistic for this is much higher. It's during this period that we often get the frustrating and victim-blaming comments of 'Why do you go back if the relationship is so bad?' or 'Just leave them for good this time'. These comments go a long way to prove that society is yet to fully embrace the true extent of trauma bonding, which is why I felt compelled to dedicate a book to the topic. I felt unbelievably alone and misunderstood when I would return to my abuser, and to have some way to show that I wasn't to blame for my situation would have been helpful for me during this time. What would have been especially beneficial for me would have been more readily available materials on the addiction victims have to their abuser. This would have helped me feel less shame about the addiction (knowing it's something other victims endure too) and it would have helped clue me up on what I was experiencing.

Like the way Stockholm Syndrome manifests, the victim of the abuse bonds with their abuser as both the source of fear and comfort in an attempt to survive the relationship. As a result, the victim then feels a misplaced yet unwavering sense of loyalty and commitment to their abusers, which to an uneducated outsider often appears utterly nonsensical. Trauma bonding is usually exceptionally fierce in situations where there are repetitive cycles of abuse. This often results in the victim having a desire to rescue their abuser, to free them from the thing inside them that causes them to behave so toxically. This desperate want to help change their abuser for the better is often present in the victim, no matter how much they've been betrayed by their abuser. However, during this need to repair a broken narcissist or make them 'better', the victim is likely going through cognitive dissonance.

Cognitive dissonance is a psychological term that describes the emotional confusion that victims experience when in a relationship with a narcissist; it's not something that occurs in healthy relationships.

It is a common defense mechanism that the victim will use to cope with the deception, lies, control and abuse that occurs in a narcissistic relationship. The cognitive dissonance then results from the victim having two highly conflicting thoughts at the same time, or from partaking in behavior that conflicts with their core beliefs or values.

The concept of cognitive dissonance is offered in its title: 'Cognitive' refers to your thinking (or your mind), and 'dissonance' is referring to the inconsistencies and conflicts that are filling your thoughts.

Cognitive dissonance is the emotional confusion and discomfort you experience when you are keeping hold of two conflicting ideas simultaneously. Naturally, we don't like the discomfort of conflicting thoughts. This theory suggests that when this occurs, we have a motivational drive within us that allows us to rationalize and change our attitudes, values, and actions - anything that allows us to reduce or erode the dissonance that we are experiencing.

For example, someone who is being beaten by their abusive spouse will despise and resent the conditions they are living in. However, with a consuming fear of a violent reprisal from their abuser, if they considered leaving, the fear of the consequences would likely make them choose to stay put.

The cognitive dissonance shows itself here through rationalization of the truth and denial: On the one hand, the victim detests their unhealthy relationship and all the pain that goes with it - we'll call this the 'truth' of the situation. On the other hand, the victim tells themselves that their abuser only gets angry and fights with them about things because deep down, they love and care for them - this is the denial part of the dissonance. This reframing of blatant abuse as a dysfunctional way of showing 'love and care' is simply an extreme case of denial.

Cognitive dissonance can manifest itself in a way that allows the victim of this situation to convince themselves that the relationship is still in the idealization stage when, in reality, it has moved into the stage of devaluation. It can also allow the victim to push the blame for the injustices in the relationship away from their abuser (due to fear of reprisal) to either themselves or another victim. It also helps in hiding the shame of being in such a dysfunctional relationship. This inner dialogue then reduces the anxiety felt by the victim, further enabling a trauma bond to develop.

The result is an overwhelmingly draining conflict between the victim's emotional self and their logical, rational, and reasoning self. Their cognitive dissonance their inner emotional disharmony that has arisen because of two conflicting ideas going on at the same time: the victim knows full well that they should get out of the abusive relationship, but they also know doing so could put them in danger and potential hardship.

Using the cognitive dissonance theory, the decision that decides which path the victim goes down is most likely to be the one that causes the least emotional stress. To reduce the dissonance they feel, the victim will pick the path of least resistance, and their motivational drive for inner calm will support their beliefs and justify any decisions that help them stay safe.

As you can imagine, cognitive dissonance can cause a lot of irrational decision making as the person here struggles to reconcile the two conflicting beliefs they have. On top of this, to support their irrational decision to stay in an abusive relationship, the victim tends to make heavy commitments and huge investments that almost serves to cement them into a bad relationship forever. There are a few methods of investment the victim may utilize to help reduce their cognitive dissonance:

Family Investments: The victim feels that investing everything in their abusive partner is the only way they can find to keep the family together.

Monetary Investments: Narcissists, and abusers in general, typically seek to control the family's financial situation. Trapped by this control of money, the victim finds themselves stuck in this position, often waiting for a better financial situation to come about so that they can eventually detach from their abuser. In my case, I would tell myself, if I had X amount of money, I'd be out of here - but I don't, so I'm staying put.

Lifestyle Investments: Due to having to share financial security with the abuser (willingly or not), the victim may fear losing their lifestyle, either for themselves or their children. So, they will stay because of their fear of the poverty trap that may await them if they leave.

Intimacy Investments: Abusers often use the blackmail of intimacy against their partner. Finding themselves in a seemingly hopeless situation and feeling broken, the victim feels the only way for them to feel 'okay' is for them to stay.

Whilst experiencing cognitive dissonance, the victim can adopt a pattern of denial, diversion, and defensiveness to help them control their discomfort. To survive, they mentally scramble to find ways of reducing their anxiety-inducing cognitive dissonance. The strategies they may use in an attempt to do this include lying to themselves to justify their behavior and even regressing into infantile patterns of acting.

Infantile Regression is an unconscious defense mechanism that is triggered when a person is exposed to terror. Narcissists often not only render their victims to horrific emotional terror but also to physical terror; this terror that must be denied by the victim if they are to survive the onslaught of abuse they are exposed to over time.

Clawing to survive under these traumatic conditions, the victim is reduced to becoming much like an infant, a small being that is helpless and dependent, its survival in the hands of their main caregiver. As you know, this usually begins with the infant's parent (usually the mother), but in this situation, the caregiver is the victim's spouse. Nature is a magical thing; it pre-programs the infant with survival instincts by providing it with a need to bond with their primary caregiver. However, in this case, it's much less innocent and born from trauma and horrifying experiences endured by the victim.

For an infant's first emotional attachment in a scary world, they bond with someone who offers the attributes for ensuring their survival: a caregiver that shows a sense of power, safety, security, and compassion. In essence, every child almost goes through the same kind of emotions that Stockholm Syndrome provokes, as a natural defense mechanism against its own demise.

Pull Yourself Out of the Toxic Bond

We've established that trauma bonds are addictive. They produce brain chemicals that are hard to overcome. When people get involved in relationships that are toxic, they become hooked on the good experiences their spouse can bring into their lives. Breaking that addiction is essentially overcoming the undeniably strong brain chemistry created by powerful and emotional experiences. It's hard to do when it feels like your mind is working against all logic and reason.

Trauma bonds are stronger than typical human bonds - think of a trauma bond as the giant Goliath of a bond. Where a person ends a relationship that was bonded without the added complexity of trauma, the pain of the break-up is much less intense and painful than it is for those who are traumatically bonded. Breaking this bond requires a lot more work - but I want to show you that you can break free.

By reading this far, I think you've certainly begun the process of breaking the addiction to your abuser; simply filling your mind with an understanding of the bond you're in is a giant step towards a healthier direction.

By opening yourself up to materials like this book, you will hopefully think about your own feelings about your situation once you've put it down. This thinking and exposing yourself to the difficult reality of the relationship helps you to identify your real feelings.

To nudge you closer to thinking more about the truth of your situation, I want you to recognize the relationships "crazy cycle". For example, my crazy cycle was: **anticipation – some kind of affection – momentary bliss – abuse occurs - confusion – the departure of my abuser – longing – utter despair.** Be aware that this is just my example; you ought to identify your own cycle within your relationship. This may be similar or even identical to mine, but taking the time to think about your cycle is helpful in this process.

I would really encourage you to write down your cycle, along with what is being fulfilled in your toxic relationship (a sense of having a family, feeling wanted, feeling secure, etc.) Notice that you're only temporarily being fulfilled; the rest of the time is full of uncertainty, angst, pain, and sadness. I find writing things down to be incredibly cathartic, and it's served me well as not only a post-break-up form of therapy but jotting my feelings down really served to help guide me through understanding the toxic bond I was in, too.

I'd also like you to determine obsessive thoughts. This was something I was advised to do from another survivor who had endured years of abuse from her ex. She had moved on from that toxic relationship, but she was still an active member of an online community for abuse victims. She was a pool of knowledge on the subject of recovery, and she offered me some fantastic advice on utilizing writing exercises to help me understand and overcome my feelings. When she first asked me to 'figure out the obsessive thoughts I had,' I told her I had none. I told her I wasn't obsessive in the slightest - I was simply in a toxic relationship I couldn't get out of. For some reason, the thought of being addicted to my abuser made me feel utterly stupid, and I denied that being a possibility for so long. 'Obsessive' had such negative connotations to me that I didn't want to associate myself with that word. Gently, my mentor eventually got me to see sense and stop being so proud that I couldn't face my own feelings. In the end, I wrote down all the obsessive thoughts I was having regarding my toxic spouse. For example, I was obsessed with preventing another cheating episode from happening. I was obsessed with making my abuser the person they were when we met. I would obsess over our first few months together, as it felt perfect. I'd obsess over the time he punched me in the face and left me locked in the house alone for two days. I'd obsess over the time it took him in the bathroom for fear of him calling up another woman whilst he was in there. The list was extremely long by the time I'd finished. I'd like you to try this exercise, too.

It's important for you to commit to yourself to live in the truth. Addictive relationships where a trauma bond has developed are just fantasies. I want to remind you that you are in love with what you wish the other person was - you're not in love with who your partner is. You're in love with an idea, a memory, a fantasy; it's not real.

Again, I felt stupid when this was explained to me - I felt dumb, like a child who still believed in Santa way past the age they should. I would often deny my real feelings because I didn't want to accept that I was in a toxic relationship, but also because I found it too difficult to admit that I was still in that relationship because I chose to believe an alternate reality.

However, I had no reason to feel so stupid; there's a lot of brain chemistry involved in creating and maintaining a trauma bond. We are addicted to the brain chemistry attached to the anticipation and bonding surrounding the relationship. Because the relationship is so completely unfulfilling for us, we are left in a constant state of emptiness, which is temporarily decreased with each encounter with our object of obsession. Here's probably the most difficult thing you're going to hear: To heal, you must abstain from your addiction. To recover means to abstain from the relationship completely - this means zero contact at all. This is the only way you can break the bond. You must detach. You need to prize yourself away from the unfulfilling emotional entanglements of the relationship.

I understand that this will be a very difficult part of your journey. For a long time would complain that I couldn't do it, that it was too hard to leave my abuser. The brain chemicals that are released when you try to detach are vastly different from the ones released when you are with your partner - almost the direct opposite. This can make it so very hard to commit to detaching yourself from your abuser.

The main chemical, as I mentioned earlier, that is released during times of emotional stress is Cortisol. Any trigger that evokes an emotionally stressful reaction (such as the loss of a loved one) releases chemicals, including the release of Cortisol As you face another emotional departure from your spouse, your system goes into overdrive, releasing stress chemicals into your body, motivating you do something about the emotional distress you're going through. As you foresee the relief from the stress, your brain releases the chemicals that counteract the Cortisol, such as Dopamine, which offers the positive feelings of anticipation. This is the 'craving' part of the addiction.

In order to break an addiction, you need to understand that you are battling these chemical responses. This does mean that by severing the relationship, you will not feel very good for a while; like any addict breaking their addiction, withdrawals are to be expected. Rest assured, just like any other addiction, if you can refuse to respond to your brain chemistry, you will get through these incredibly tough times, and your brain will eventually come to rest at a state of balance and calmness.

Here are my suggestions to help you emotionally break away from a trauma bond when you're enduring the "craving cycle."

#1: Find a positive distraction; find something positive to do with your craving energy – reading, writing, walking, meditating, or any other activity that you feel you could enjoy (or used to enjoy). My distraction was walking the dog and reading. I know that you'll rarely feel like doing anything other than obsessing over your abuser and craving their comfort, but I promise you that if you drag yourself up and try to do something that diverts your attention away from them, you'll begin to feel better. Not immediately, but eventually. Your mind will slowly be edging away from your constant, obsessive thoughts and onto healthier things. Even if you read about things like this; narcissism, abuse, or unhealthy relationships. Whilst it's not the most feel-good topic, it means you're educating yourself and retaining a logical approach to your situation. When I was pining after my ex, I found books like this a comfort, but I also strived to make sure I had other distractions that had nothing at all to do with my toxic relationship (such as walking the dog whilst listening to music).

Doing physical things, even when you don't feel like lifting your head from your pillow, is incredibly beneficial when you're fixated on your abuser. Eventually, after a couple of months without my abuser, I began going to exercise classes with an old coworker who I got back in touch with after the break-up. I can't stress how much those Tuesday and Thursday night sessions helped me; not only did it get me out of the house, it helped me feel better about myself, gave me the socialization I desperately needed, and helped build my confidence.

#2: Try to connect with someone healthy. This can be hard if your abuser has segregated you away from all of your close family and friends, but once you've ended the toxic partnership, you'll be pleasantly surprised with the number of people you can reconnect with. From old school friends to coworkers from a decade ago to a close friend who you've drifted away from; these people are often more open to reconnecting with you than you'd imagine.

Just talking to people really opens your mind. After being in such a suppressive relationship for so long, I was eager to hear what other people lived like. What they did for work, how they enjoyed their evenings, how they spent their weekends, and what they did with their free time - all of this was alien to me at the time because I'd been wrapped tightly in a trauma bond. Every day had been the same for me, and to hear the exciting possibilities life could now hold for me was something I got from talking to people who had healthy relationships.

If you're lucky enough to have a close friend or circle of friends, then reach out to them and get some healthy conversation going - even if the conversation reverts back to your abuser (we all need to talk about it from time to time, particularly during this phase), then so be it. As long as the entire conversation isn't about your relationship, then you can get some emotional goodness from having a healthy conversation.

#3: Write in a journal. I know I've mentioned this earlier, but I can't stress how soothing and healing writing things down can be. Journaling or even simply jotting your feelings down is so effective for releasing uncomfortable and unwanted emotions. Write about how you feel and what you want out of life.

It also helps to purge toxicity if you write a list of all the reasons your addictive relationship is bad for you. It's incredibly easy to only focus on what you miss when you are going through feelings of emptiness, but it will serve to strengthen your resolve if you can focus on the negative aspects of your relationship. This will help line you up with reality.

Also, be sure to encourage yourself in your journal - you're going through a tough, testing time - don't forget to remind yourself that you've endured a lot and can come out of this bigger and better.

Your Recovery Dos and Don'ts Checklist:

- I will trust my intuition.

You must trust your own gut instincts - you've been stripped of your trust in your own intuitions, but this is no longer the case. You must now take heed of what your gut is telling you.

- I will no longer partake in "impossible situations."

Not only do impossible situations not serve you, but they also aim to keep you downtrodden. Your duty to yourself is to make sure you no longer actively partake in these demoralizing situations.

- I will take one day at a time.

Taking your life one day at a time ensures you're taking little steps every day towards becoming healed. Don't worry about next week or months down the line - take each day as it comes. Then, when the future arrives, you haven't wasted your time worrying about it, you've lived in the now.

- When I'm feeling anxious, I will not panic myself with negative thoughts. I will encourage myself with positive thoughts instead.

Whatever anxieties you're confronted with, there is no power in negative thinking. You won't find solutions or comfort in negative thinking. Replace those toxic thoughts with positive ones: you will find a solution to anything, and if you don't, things have a way of working themselves our anyway - don't dwell, don't waste your time on negative energy and don't feed your anxiety.

- I will manage my emotions rather than having them control me.

This one does take practice, but practice makes perfect. Instead of being controlled and manipulated by your own emotions (many of which will have been instilled into you by your abuser), learn to control your emotions. Know what triggers you and find ways to stop it from controlling your thoughts and actions.

- I will take back my power.

The power you handed over to your abuser and the power they so callously stripped you of isn't gone forever. Your power isn't unreplenishable.

- I will believe in myself.

This one speaks for itself. You are capable of so much if you believe in yourself.

- If I feel emotionally unstable, I will not try to connect with the object of my obsession.

This will be a case of five steps backward if you do. You'll get a temporary comfort (maybe), but then you'll be right back at the first step in the cycle of abuse. If you feel emotionally unstable, distract yourself, and if you have someone you can talk to, reach out to them. Under no circumstances will you try to reconnect with your abuser.

- I will have compassion for myself and pay attention to my feelings.

Self-hatred is a common side effect when you're in an abusive relationship. You can't heal unless you show yourself some compassion; you're human, you will make mistakes. It's how you handle them and learn from them that matters. Don't dwell on the things you've done or the person the relationship turned you into. You deserve compassion from yourself.

- I endeavor to build a brand new "toxicity free" life for myself.

Your life is yours to build. You don't have to live suppressed, unhappy, miserable, afraid, anxious, or without dreams. Build your own nirvana.

- I will enjoy the rest of my life. I will remind myself that no matter what I've been through, life can be good.

Life can be unbelievably good. So can people. It may seem so far away, but genuinely feeling good is within your reach, but you can't grasp the happiness you deserve while you're in the constant toxic loop of the trauma bond.

Things to Remember on Your Recovery Journey

The power of the trauma bond is unlike any other connection you'll feel towards another person in your entire life. It's an all-consuming, utterly engulfing pit of emotional purgatory.

I still recall the time when my ex shifted from his love bombing and constant adoration of me towards being colder and more distant. The heart-sinking panic you feel when your abuser shifts from adoring you to seemingly being annoyed by your actions and treating you like you're an inconvenience to them drives you crazy. The thought that my 'perfect' partner was drifting away from me - that I was driving him away - filled me with dread. I couldn't bear to think about life without him, and so I would do anything to claw him back and make him stay; even endure the most horrific episodes of abuse.

Such was the strength of the trauma bond I was bound so tightly in, I even *begged* my abuser to stay with me when I found out he had been seeing someone else. To him, it was a 'one-time thing' that was brought on because I'd 'driven him to it.' So, he was justifying his own actions by minimizing the effects of them (saying it was just a one-time event) and then gaslighting me and heaping the blame onto me. Of course, the strength of this toxic bond means I took on that blame. And I believed it.

My ex would also frequently disappear for days on end. Sometimes I would find out the hurtful, deceitful things he did; most of the time I wouldn't. The only way I would find out the humiliating things he'd been up to was social media - his social media. I would only know what he would allow me to know, and if he wanted to hurt me, he'd put pictures online that he knew would hurt me. The intent of these posts was indeed to make me feel upset and panic that I was losing him for good, but at the time, I couldn't fathom that. By the time my ex would return home from his bender, I'd be beside myself with a tonne of emotions - I'd be relieved he came back, I'd be utterly devastated by the things he'd done, and I'd also be incredibly angry that he did those things. If you roll all of those emotions up into one, mix them with anxiety and panic, and you get one incredibly unhinged individual. And that's what I become. I'd cry, I'd plead with him, and I'd go crazy with the fear of losing him. I'd rather be with him and endure the hell-like abuse than be without him; it seemed the lesser of two evils.

My ex would turn up at my workplace and humiliate me, accusing me of having affairs with my colleagues or would just be incredibly rude to the people I worked with. I'd be left mortified, but I'd still try and justify his behavior to my coworkers, sticking up for him and desperately explaining away his actions. Most people couldn't comprehend why I was still with him when he treated me with such vulgar disrespect, and ironically, people not understanding my relationship pushed me further towards him.

The reality is those who've never had the first-hand experience of a trauma bond tend to find it difficult to fully wrap their head around the complexities, inconsistencies, and illogicalness of it all. For people like you and me, however, the reality of a trauma bond is ever prevalent, and we know more than anybody just how entirely crippling it is. We know it's not black and white.

It's easy to lose yourself on your recovery journey. So, anytime you feel lost, upset, guilty, or pining for your abuser, I want you to remember these things and repeat them to yourself as affirmations:

1. **I have no more energy to give to people who harm me.**

1. **My emotional health is infinitely more important than supplying power to someone else's ego.**

1. **My newfound clarity will guide me.**

1. **I'm becoming rational and logical, which is why I am reading this book to begin with.**

1. **I am worthy of happiness.**

******

I do hope this book has helped you, inspired you, given you new things to think about, and offered you some words of comfort.

Do let us know if this has been beneficial for you; you can leave a review, and if you'd like to offer up a little of your own story with it, that would be unbelievably valuable to someone who reads it who's in an abusive relationship. You can also find us on Instagram @escapethenarcs - we reply to all DM's, so feel free to get in touch. We are building our community of survivors and thrivers and welcome you to join.

Also by Lauren Kozlowski

About the Publisher

Escape The Narcissist is about helping you find your self-worth, offering you some thought provoking ideas to change your life and aiding you in revitalizing your relationships.

With that in mind, Escape The Narcissist has one core relationship we want to focus on: the one you have with yourself.

Our website was born from a place of darkness. We've all, at some point in our lives, been on the receiving end of ill treatment from others. From being a victim of a narcissistic relationship to being mistreated by those who should protect us and not being shown the respect we deserve, these toxic relationships can affect us more than we realise.

Whilst the people behind the content of our site and books all have their own ideas and stories, they have one thing in common: they've all overcome toxicity in their lives and want to share their story.

The content of the stories, pieces of advice and actionable life changes within this site all aim to inspire, provoke a healthier way of thinking, and help to heal any negative effects you've been left with at the hands of other people.

escapethenarcissist.com

CPSIA information can be obtained
at www.ICGtesting.com
Printed in the USA
LVHW101935040522
717814LV00008B/275